Silver Burdett & Ginn
SCIENCE

GEORGE G. MALLINSON
Distinguished Professor
of Science Education
Western Michigan University

JACQUELINE B. MALLINSON
Associate Professor of Science
Western Michigan University

WILLIAM L. SMALLWOOD
Head, Science Department
The Community School
Sun Valley, Idaho

CATHERINE VALENTINO
Former Director of Instruction
North Kingstown School Department
North Kingstown, Rhode Island

SILVER BURDETT & GINN
LEXINGTON, MA • MORRISTOWN, NJ
Atlanta, GA • Cincinnati, OH • Dallas, TX • Menlo Park, CA • Northfield, IL

THE SILVER BURDETT & GINN
ELEMENTARY SCIENCE PROGRAM

Pupil Books Levels 1-6
Teacher Editions Levels K-6

© 1987 Silver, Burdett & Ginn Inc. All Rights Reserved. Printed in the United States of America. This publication, or parts thereof, may not be reproduced in any form by photographic, electronic, mechanical, or any other method, for any use, including information storage and retrieval, without written permission from the publisher.
ISBN 0-382-13436-2

Silver Burdett & Ginn

SCIENCE

Contents

The Adventure of Science

What Is Science?

It is a way to ask questions about our world.

It is a way to answer our questions.

B

What Will I Learn in Science?

I will learn to ask questions.

I will learn how to find answers.

I will learn to think.

How Does Science Help Me?
I use science every day.
I know what animals need to live.
I know what makes a kite fly high.
I can tell when soup is too hot to eat.

Hot or Not?

How can I tell if something is hot?
There is a potato in the box.
It might be a hot baked potato.
It might not be hot at all.
I can find out if things are hot.
I can think of a test.

The Owl and the Mouse

What is happening here?

What are the owl and mouse doing?

F

What is happening now?
What is the owl doing?

What is the mouse doing?

How have the baby animals changed?
What do these owls eat?

What do these mice eat?
How do you know?

H

Why is the owl flying toward the mouse?
Why do you think that?
What do you think will happen next?

What happened?

J

1

Animals
of Long Ago

Long ago these animals lived on the earth.
Some were small and others were very large.
Some ate meat and others ate plants.
Can you name any of them?

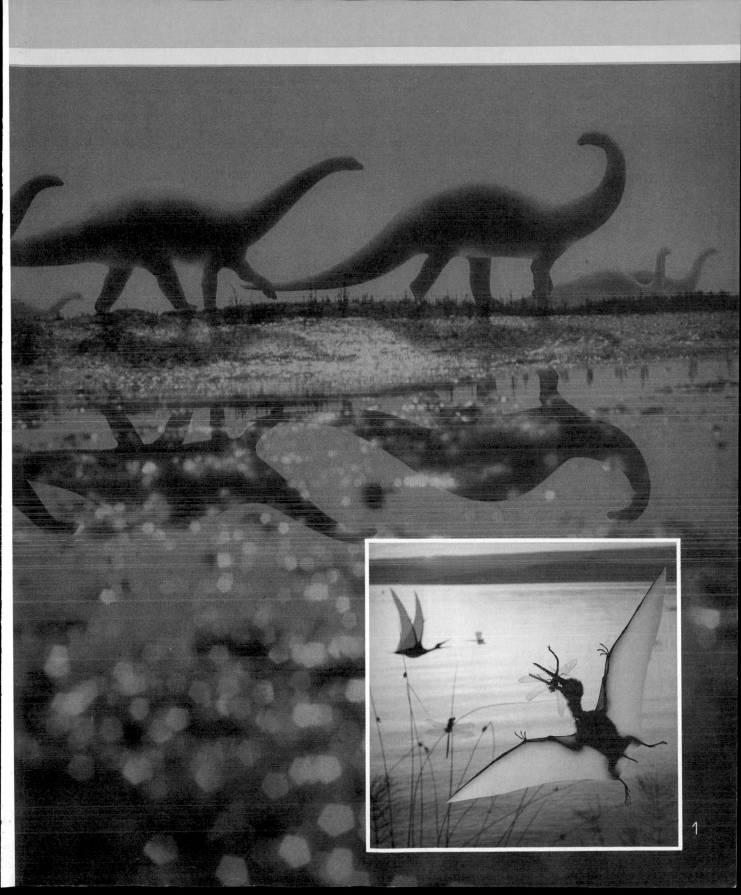

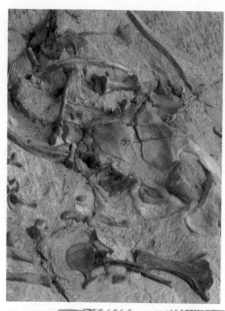

Looking for Dinosaurs

We know dinosaurs lived long ago.
People find bones in the ground.
People also find dinosaur teeth
and eggs.
The bones, teeth, and eggs help us
learn about dinosaurs.
What bones do you think these are?

People fit the bones together.

The bones show how dinosaurs looked.

They show how big dinosaurs were.

How are these dinosaurs different?

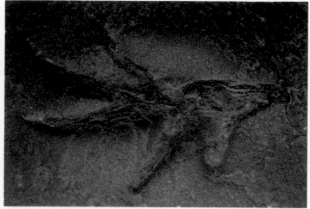

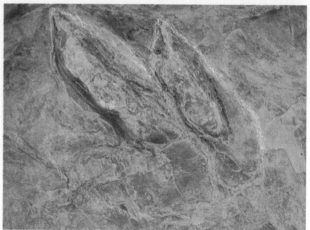

Dinosaurs often walked where the
ground was muddy.
They made **footprints** in the mud.
After many years the mud turned
into rock.
The footprints were left in the rock.
Do these footprints look alike?
How do they look different?

How are prints different?

- Flatten a ball of clay.
- Press one hand into the clay.

- Look at your handprint.
- Look at your friends' handprints.

How are their prints different from yours? What can we learn from prints?

The Land of the Dinosaurs

Dinosaurs lived where the land was warm and wet.

Part of the land was covered with water.

Many plants grew on the land.

A place like this is called a **swamp**.

There were no people on earth then.

There were no roads or buildings.

Are there places like this today?

Could dinosaurs live on earth today?

tyrannosaurus rex

The Meat Eaters

These dinosaurs lived on land.
They had sharp teeth for eating meat.
They had strong hind legs for running.
They had short front legs with
pointed claws.
How did they use their front legs?

This was the largest meat eater.
Its jaws were very strong.
It was taller than a two-story house.

ornitholestes

This dinosaur could run very fast.
It was the size of an adult person.
What do you think it ate?

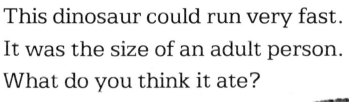

allosaurus

This dinosaur had a large head.
It also had a long tail.

It could catch dinosaurs three times
its size.

The Plant Eaters

These dinosaurs ate plants.
They had many flat teeth.
They used these teeth to grind food.
They walked on four legs.

This dinosaur was as long as three
school buses.
It ate plants growing near water.

apatosaurus

10

stegosaurus

This dinosaur had thick skin.

It also had a spiked tail.

How do you think it used its tail?

triceratops

This dinosaur had horns on its head.

A large flat bone covered its neck.

How do you think it used its horns?

pterodactyl

rhamphorhynchus

Other Animals of Long Ago

Other animals lived long ago.

Some of them could fly.

They had claws on their wings.

They ate smaller animals.

How did they use their claws?

Some animals lived in the sea.
They had flippers to help them swim.
Many were shaped like fish.
What animals today look like these?

plesiosaur

ichthyosaur

13

How does a dinosaur skeleton look?

- Put two pipe cleaners together like this.
- Bend them to make a skull and spine.
- Bend two more pipe cleaners in half.
- Twist them around the spine for legs.
- Cut ribs and twist them around the spine.

What bones can you name on the skeleton?

What can you tell by looking at the bones?

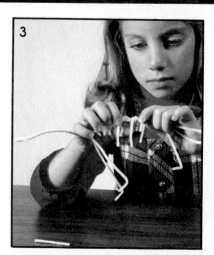

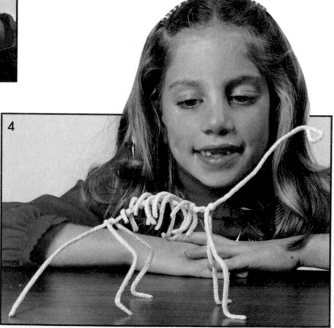

iguanodon

coelophysis

The Changing Earth

Years later the earth changed.
Many places became very dry.
Some places became very cold.
Many plants and animals died.
All the dinosaurs died, too.
No one knows why they died.
Maybe it was too cold.
Maybe there was not enough food.
What do you think happened?

15

giant bison

woolly rhinoceros

woolly mammoth

wolves

Ice and snow covered part of the earth.
Animals with thick fur lived here.
Their fur helped to keep them warm.
Many of these animals were large.

Other parts of the earth were warm.
These animals lived in warm places.
They are not living today.
What animals today look like them?

giant deer

eohippus

saber-toothed tiger

Animals in Trouble

These are animals living today.

There are not many of them left.

They are **endangered**.

This means they may die out,

just like the dinosaurs did.

Sometimes people build towns where wild animals live.

Then the animals must find new homes.

What else endangers wild animals?

How can we help to keep them alive?

Check It Now

WORDS TO KNOW

Match each word with its meaning.

1. dinosaur   a. land that is warm and wet
2. swamp   b. brown bears and green turtles
3. flippers   c. large animals that are extinct
4. meat eaters   d. body parts used for swimming
5. plant eaters   e. animals with sharp teeth
6. endangered   f. animals with flat teeth

IDEAS TO KNOW

Which of these animals are not alive today?

Which of these animals are endangered?

A   B   C   D   E

THINKING LIKE A SCIENTIST

A scientist found a bone in a dry stream.
It was a dinosaur bone 9 feet high.
Scientists studied the bone.
They think the dinosaur was over 100 feet tall.
How could they tell by looking at one bone?
Use the pictures to help you think.

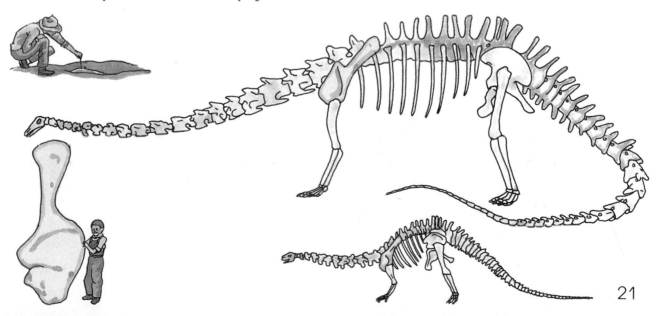

2

How Plants Grow

There are many kinds of **plants**.

Most of them grow from seeds.

Seeds can be large or small.

Plants can be large or small.

Plants change as they grow.

What changes do you see in the pictures?

Seeds

There are many kinds of **seeds**.

Each kind of seed plant makes its own kind of seeds.

This plant makes sunflower seeds.

The seeds grow into sunflower plants.

Look at the pictures below.

What plants will grow from these seeds?

Trees make seeds, too.

What kinds of trees are these?

Where do you find the seeds on these trees?

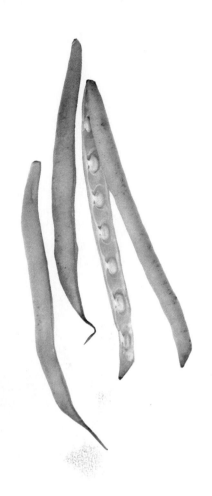

How Seeds Grow

Have you ever looked closely at a seed?
It has a cover around it.
The cover is called the **seed coat**.
It keeps the seed from drying out.
Some seeds have a hard coat.
The hard coat protects the seed.
Inside each seed is a tiny plant.
Most seeds also have stored food.

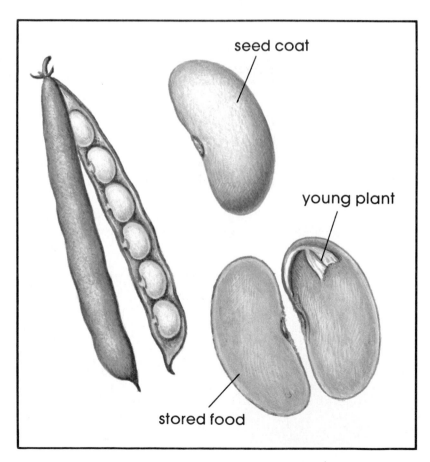

seed coat

young plant

stored food

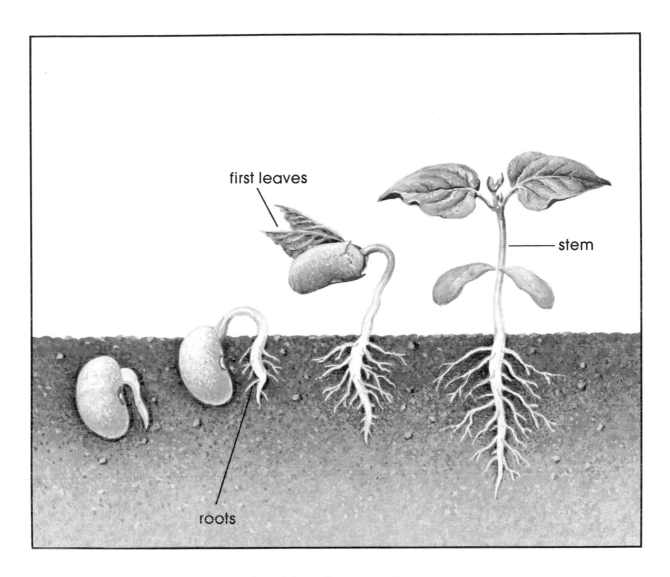

first leaves

stem

roots

The tiny plant grows inside the seed.

It uses the food stored there.

Soon it breaks through the seed coat.

Then you can see the plant parts.

The parts are **roots, stem,** and **leaves**.

Find each of these parts in the picture.

The plant changes as it grows.

The roots grow longer.

The plant stem grows longer.

More leaves grow on the stem.

Some plants grow more than one stem.

How has the plant changed?

Flowers and Fruit

Some plants have **flowers**.
Flowers have many shapes and colors.
Each kind of plant has its own kind
of flower.
Look at the pictures.
How are the flowers alike?
How are the flowers different?
Can flowers of the same kind have
different colors?
Which picture shows this?

Flowers change as the plants grow.

Many flowers change into **fruits**.

Name the fruits in the pictures.

Seeds are found inside fruits.

New plants grow from the seeds.

How can seeds be grouped?

- Look at different kinds of seeds.
- Think about how the seeds are alike.
- Put them in groups.

How did you group them?

Plants and Seasons

Plants change with the **seasons**.
Most plants grow when it is warm.
They stop growing when it is cold.
How does this tree change?

New growth begins in the **spring**.

This is when farmers plant seeds.

Other people plant seeds, too.

The seeds grow as the days get warmer.

Trees and bushes grow new leaves
and stems.

33

Plants grow through the **summer**.

Some plants make food that people eat.

Corn plants grow ears of corn.

Tomato plants grow tomatoes.

Apple trees grow apples.

What is growing in this garden?

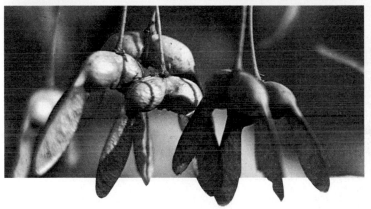

Many plants stop growing in the **fall**.

Some plants die and others rest.

Seeds are carried away by
wind and animals.

The seeds are dropped on the ground.

They stay there all **winter**.

New plants grow from some of the
seeds in the spring.

How else can seeds be carried?

Growing Plants

Plants do not always grow from seeds.

Plants can grow in other ways.

They can grow from parts of plants.

New plants can grow from stems.

New plants grow from leaves and roots.

How is this plant growing?

How does a sweet potato grow?

- Pour water into a glass.
- Put a sweet potato into the glass.
- Be sure the tip is in the water.

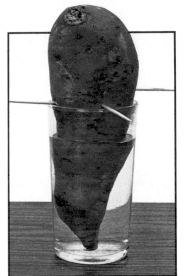

- Observe the plant each day. Does a sweet potato grow from a seed?

37

WORDS TO KNOW

Use these words to name the parts of a plant.

root   stem   leaf   flower

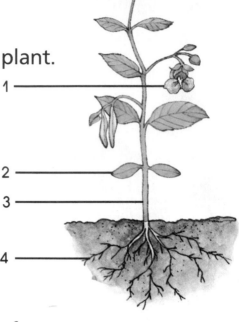

IDEAS TO KNOW

Match each seed with the plant it comes from.

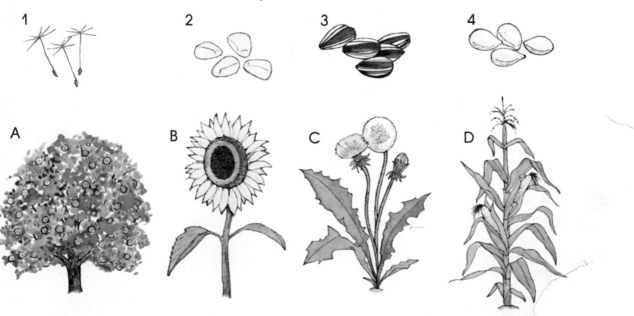

Put the pictures in order from seed to new plant.

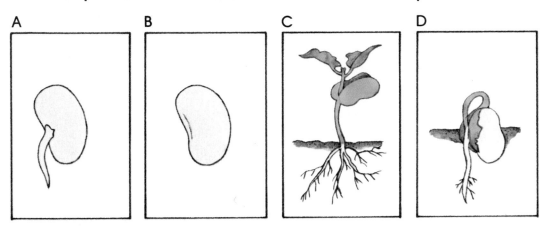

A   B   C   D

Match each seed with the fruit it comes from.

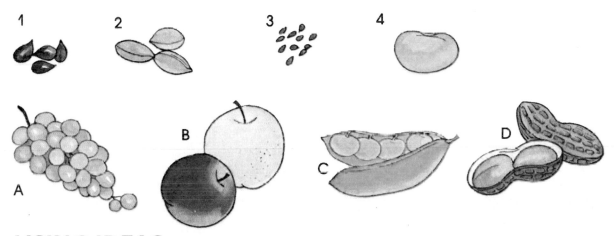

1   2   3   4

A   B   C   D

USING IDEAS

You can make a window garden from scraps.

Use the tops of carrots.

Radish and beet tops will work, too.

Put the tops in a low dish with some water.

Keep the dish near a sunny window.

Watch and see what happens.

3

Where Plants and Animals Live

Plants and animals live in many places.

They live together in most places.

Where do these plants and animals live?

Where else do plants and animals live?

Woods

Pretend we are walking in the **woods**.

Listen! Do you hear a bird chirping?

Look! A spider is spinning a web.

A squirrel is digging in the leaves.

What do you think it is looking for?

Many kinds of animals live in the woods.
Here are other animals you might see.
Where could you look to find them?
What other animals live in the woods?

Trees grow close together in the woods.
Look at their branches.
They make a roof over the ground.
Very little sunlight reaches the ground.
It is shady in the woods.

Some plants grow well in the shade.
They are found in the woods.
Many small animals live in the woods.
Some of these animals live in the trees.
Others live in the soil.
Where do the animals in the pictures live?

Some trees have large flat leaves.
Other trees have thin pointed leaves.
In the fall some trees lose
all of their leaves.
Other trees stay green all year round.
Which trees below lose their leaves?

Some plants die during the winter.

Other plants rest.

What does the woods look like in the winter?

How does it change in the spring?

Animals use plants for food and
shelter.

In places where the winter is cold,
animals cannot find enough food.
Some animals move to warmer places
to find food.

Other animals crawl into holes
and under rocks.
These animals sleep during the winter.

How can you make a place for living things?

- Get a clear plastic cup.
- Cover the bottom of the cup with pebbles.
- Put in some soil.
- Add rocks and a small cap with water.
- Put in some small plants.
- Get a cup with holes on top.
- Tape it over the top of the first cup.

What animals could live there?

49

Deserts

Pretend we are in a different kind of place.

The sun is shining brightly.

The air is hot and dry.

The soil is very sandy.

This place is a **desert**.

It is very quiet here.

Animals like these live in the desert.

Most of the animals cannot be seen
during the day.

Many of them are sleeping.

They come out at night to eat.

Why do they sleep during the day?

There is little shade in the desert.
Since it doesn't rain often, very
few trees grow here.
Look at the pictures.
What do these desert plants look like?
How are they different from plants in
the woods?

Why are leaves different in size and shape?

- Wet two paper towels with water.
- Lay one flat near a window.
- Roll up the other towel.
- Place it next to the flat towel.

What do you think will happen to the towels?

- Feel the two towels the next day.

How are the towels different?

Suppose a cactus had large flat leaves.

What would happen to water in the leaves?

How do the spines help a desert plant?

Ponds

Pretend we are visiting a **pond**.

You will find many plants and animals here.

Look! A frog is sitting on a lily pad.

There are some ducks swimming across
the pond.

Find the turtle sunning itself.

A dragonfly is flying nearby.

Cattails are growing in the pond.

Let's row a boat across the pond.

Many kinds of fish live in the pond.

Did you hear a splash?

A small tree has fallen into
the water.

A beaver is fixing its dam.

Beavers build dams of mud and branches.

How do the dams help make a pond?

Oceans

Look at the globe.

You can see that much of the earth is covered with water.

Not all the water is in lakes or ponds.

Most of the water on the earth is in **oceans**.

Ocean water is different from the water in lakes and ponds.

Ocean plants and animals are different from living things in other places.

How is ocean water different from pure water?

- Put salt water in one dish.
- Put pure water in the other dish.
- Observe the dishes in a day or two.

Where did the water go?

What do you see and feel in the dishes?

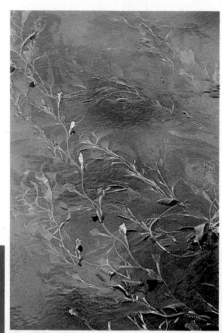

Some plants grow in the ocean.
They grow where the water is not
too deep.
Here the plants get sunlight.
Many kinds of animals live in the ocean.
Some ocean animals look like plants.
They do not move around.

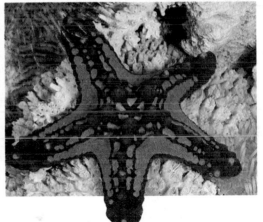

Animals in the ocean have different
shapes and colors.
Can you name any of these animals?
People use some ocean animals for food.
What food do you eat from the ocean?

Check It Now

WORDS TO KNOW

What place does each sentence tell about?

    pond   desert   woods   ocean

1. The soil here is hot and sandy.
2. Animals such as frogs and beavers live here.
3. Most of the water on the earth is here.
4. Trees make a roof over the ground here.

IDEAS TO KNOW

Match the sentences with the pictures.

1. Animals use plants for food and shelter.
2. Plants in the desert have special leaves.
3. Some plants change with the seasons.
4. Ocean plants and animals can live in salt water.

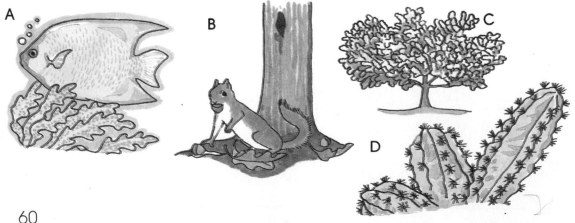

60

Tell where these animals live.

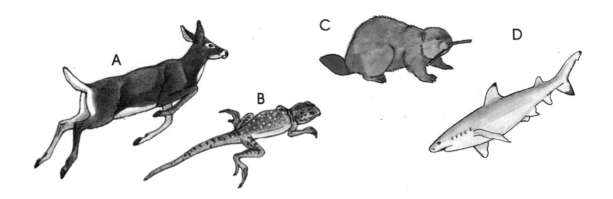

USING IDEAS

These tracks were found in the woods.

Can you find the animal that made each one?

Look around on your way to school.

What kinds of animals and plants do you see?

Draw pictures of the ones you see.

4

Things in Our World

There are many things in our world.
Some of them are living.
Some of them are not living.
How are things different?

Using Your Senses

Your senses help you learn about things.

Imagine you are at a circus.

You can see many different things.

You can see horses and elephants.

You can see someone dive into water.

You can see clowns and balloons.

Your senses tell you that things
are different.
Things at the circus have different
colors, shapes, and sizes.
But things at the circus are alike in other ways.
They all take up space and have weight.
Things that take up space and have
weight are called **matter**.

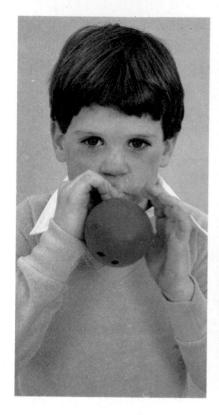  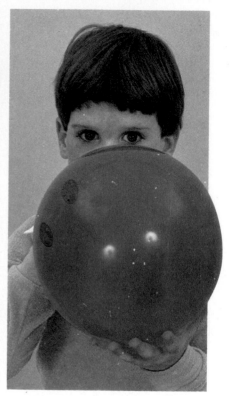

Taking Up Space

It is easy to see matter like rocks
and water.

You can see that they take up space.

You cannot see air.

It is not easy to see that air takes
up space.

What do you think the boy is putting
into the balloon?

Does it take up space in the balloon?

Does air take up space?

- Put some paper into a plastic cup.
- Hold the cup upside down in water.

What happened to the paper?

- Put a paper cup upside down into water.
- Poke a hole in the cup with a pencil.

What happened to the air?

How else can you show that air takes up space?

Things Have Weight

Everything in our world has **weight**.
Some things weigh more than others.
Size does not always tell us what
things weigh.
Some large things weigh less than
small things.
Look at the things in the pictures.
Do you know which things are heavier?
Does size help you know weight?

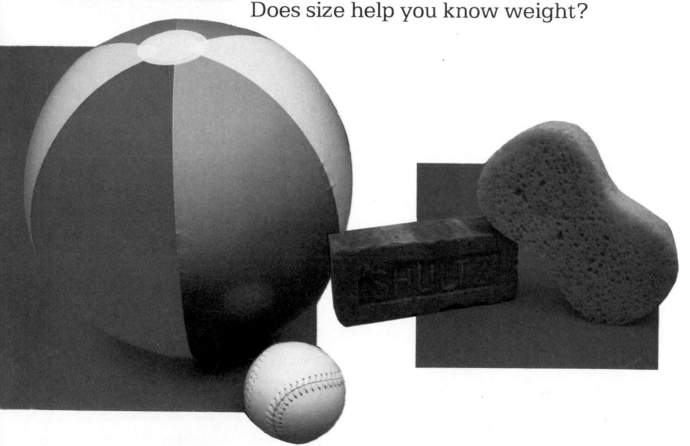

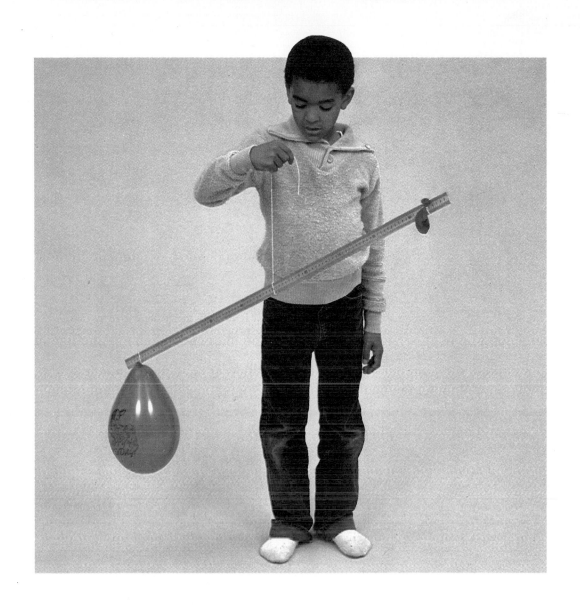

Air is in the balloons.

Matter like air is hard to weigh.

You may think it does not have weight.

Look at the picture.

Which balloon weighs more?

Does air have weight?

We can use water to compare matter.
Bubbles are made of air.
They rise in water.
Do air and water weigh the same?
What does oil do in water?
What else rises in water?

Look at the pictures below.
Do the rock and the water weigh
the same?
How do you know?
What else sinks in water?

Which things float in water?

- Fill a bowl with water.
- Get a Ping-Pong ball and a golf ball.
- Hold the two balls on the bottom.

What will happen when you let the balls go?

- Get some other things to try.

What will happen when you put the objects into the water?

- Try each one.

Grouping Matter

People put matter into three groups.
Each group is different.
The first group is like rocks.
The things in the picture belong in this group.
They do not change shape when they are moved.
These things are called **solids**.
A solid is a kind of matter.
What other solids can you name?

The next group of matter you see is
like water.

This matter does not have a shape of
its own.

Milk, juice, and oil are in this group.

They change their shape when they
are poured.

They are called **liquids**.

How have these liquids changed?

The last group is like **air**.
You cannot see air.
Air does not have a shape of its own.
Matter like air is called a **gas**.
How do you know there is air in the balloons?

What happens if air is let out of
a balloon?
It spreads out to fill a larger space.
Air can also be pumped into small spaces.
What changes do you see in the pictures?

We know that all matter is alike in
two ways.
It takes up space and has weight.
Which of these takes up the most space?
Which of these has the most weight?

We know that matter can be grouped
in three ways.
The three groups are solids, liquids,
and gases.
In which group does each of the
things in the pictures belong?

Changing Matter

Some matter can change from one group to another.

Liquids can change to solids.

Liquid water can change to ice.

Liquids can also change to gases.

How has the water in the picture changed?

How does matter change?

- Wipe a wet sponge across a chalkboard.

What do you think will happen to the water?

- Wait a few minutes.

What has happened to the water?

- Mix the orange juice with water.
- Pour it into an ice tray.
- Put it in the freezer.

What happens to the juice?

WORDS TO KNOW

Fill in the missing word in each sentence.
Use the pictures to help you.

solid   liquid    gas

1. Ice is a _____ that can change to a liquid.

2. Air is a clear _____ that takes up space.

3. A _____, such as water, can change to a solid.

IDEAS TO KNOW

How many living and nonliving things can you find?

Read each sentence. Draw a picture of matter
to go with each sentence.

1. It has weight.
2. It takes up space.
3. It has its own shape.
4. It takes the shape of its container.
5. It spreads out to fill larger spaces.
6. It floats in water.

USING IDEAS

What did you eat for breakfast today?

Make a list.

Name the liquids.

Name the solids.

THINKING LIKE A SCIENTIST

New bags of cereal and crackers are puffed
out with air.

How does the air protect
the food?

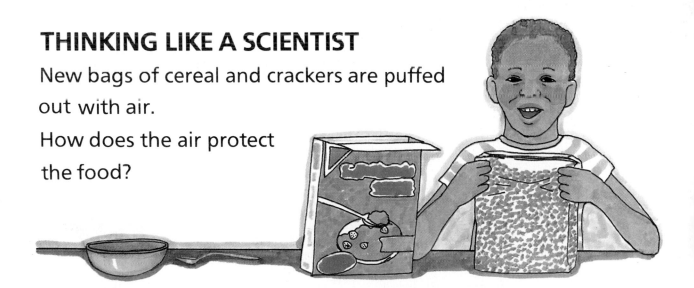

5

Fun with Magnets

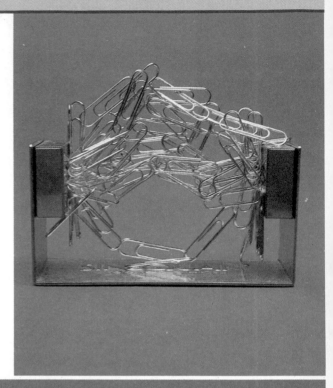

There are many kinds of **magnets**.
Most magnets are made by people.
Others are found in the ground.
What can magnets do?

Magnets Attract

Magnets **attract** some objects.
This means magnets can pick up
or pull some objects.

What kinds of matter does a magnet attract?

- Collect objects like these.

Which ones will a magnet attract?

- Write your guesses on a chart.
- Test each object.
- Put the objects into two groups.
- Circle the names of the objects on
  the chart that the magnet attracts.

How many of your guesses were correct?

I Predict	
Attracts	Does Not Attract
nail	crayon
eraser	
pin	

Group A
Attracts

Group B
Does Not Attract

Magnets attract through other things.
A magnet can attract through water
and paper.

Can a magnet attract through
a piece of wood?
Can it attract through plastic?

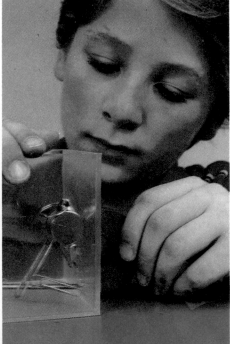

What is this child doing?

Where is the paper clip?
Where is the magnet?
Can a magnet attract
through glass?

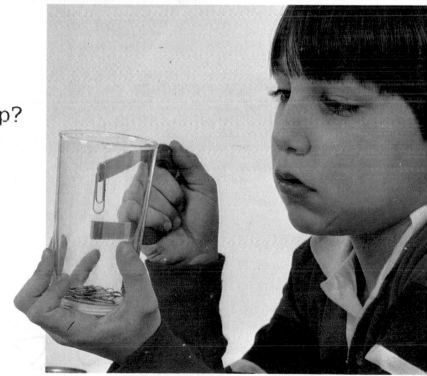

Poles

Magnets have **poles**.

They are at the ends of this magnet.

The N is for the north pole.

The S is for the south pole.

All magnets have a north pole and
a south pole.

Look at these magnets.

Where would you find the poles?

Point to the poles.

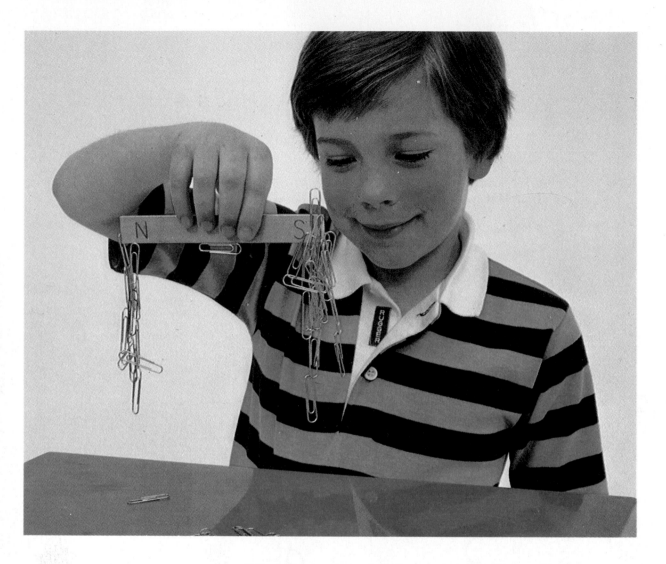

The boy is picking up paper clips
with a magnet.
Where are most of the paper clips?
What parts of this magnet are the
strongest?

How can you tell the shape of a magnet?

- Have a partner tape a magnet inside a shoebox.
- Tape the box closed.
- Do not look inside the box.
- Try to find the shape of the magnet.
- Use what you know about magnets to help you.

How did you find the shape?

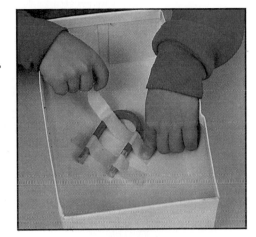

91

Two poles that are alike **repel** each other.
This means they push away from each other.
Two poles that are not alike attract
each other.

 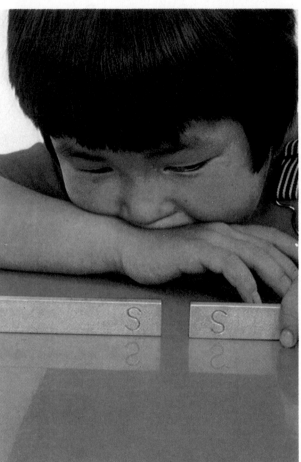

Two N poles repel each other.
Will two S poles repel each other?
Will an N pole attract or repel an S
pole?

How can you name the poles of a magnet?

- Tie a string to a magnet.
- Bring the end of another magnet near the N pole.

Do the ends attract or repel each other?

- Try this with the other end of the magnet.

What happens?

- Mark the ends of the magnet N and S.

What is another way you can find the N and S poles?

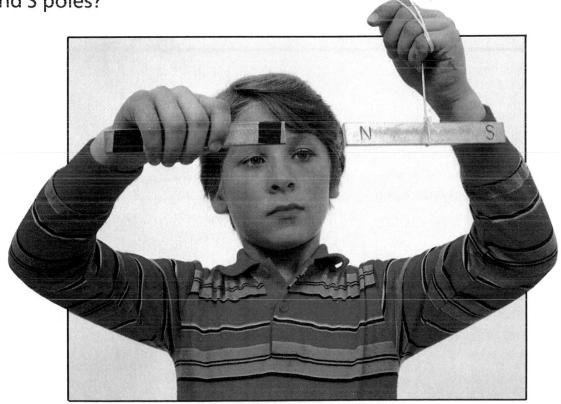

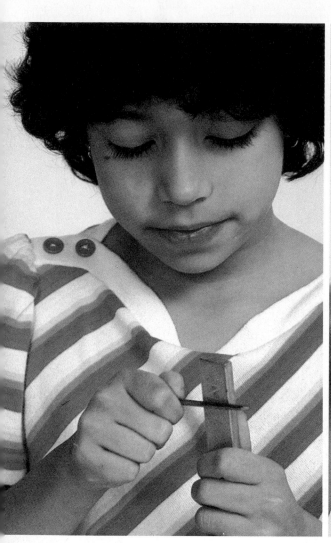
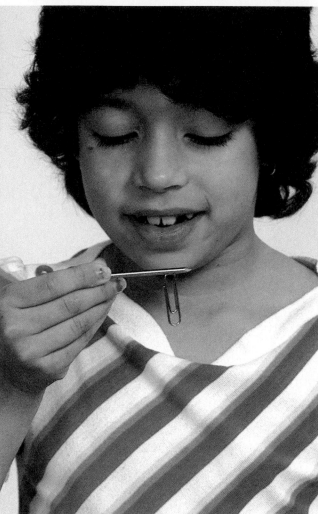

Make a Magnet

A nail can become a magnet.

It will attract other matter.

This girl has made a nail into a magnet.

She rubbed the nail with the magnet.

What other kinds of objects can

become magnets?

How can you make a magnet?

- Rub scissors 20 times with a magnet.
- Rub the same way each time.
- Pick up a paper clip with the scissors.

What other things do the scissors attract?

How many paper clips can the scissors pick up?

How many paper clips can a bar magnet pick up?

Which is stronger?

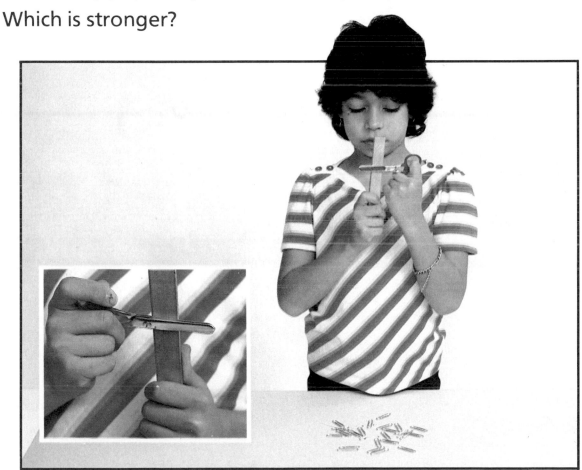

Uses

Magnets have many uses.

Magnets can help hold things.

Magnets can help lift things.

How are these magnets being used?
What are other ways magnets
can be used?

Check It Now

WORDS TO KNOW

Choose one of these words to complete each sentence.

poles   attract   repel   magnet

1. A _____ is an object that can attract other objects.

2. A magnet is strongest at its N and S _____.

3. Like poles of a magnet _____ each other.

4. Unlike poles of a magnet _____ each other.

IDEAS TO KNOW

Write the letters of the things a magnet will attract.

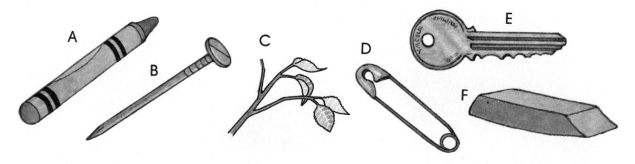

Match the picture with the sentence.

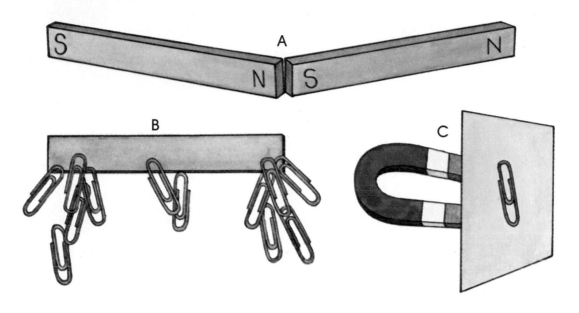

1. The poles are the strongest parts of a magnet.
2. A magnet will attract things through paper.
3. Unlike poles attract.

THINKING LIKE A SCIENTIST

This builder is using a magnet to find something.

She needs to find the wooden beams inside the wall.

The walls are nailed to the beams.

Magnets do not attract wood.

How would a magnet help?

6

Heat
and Light

Heat and **light** are two kinds of **energy**. We can see light energy. We can feel heat energy. Some light energy comes from the sun. When sunlight strikes the earth, it changes to heat. Without the sun the earth would be cold and dark.

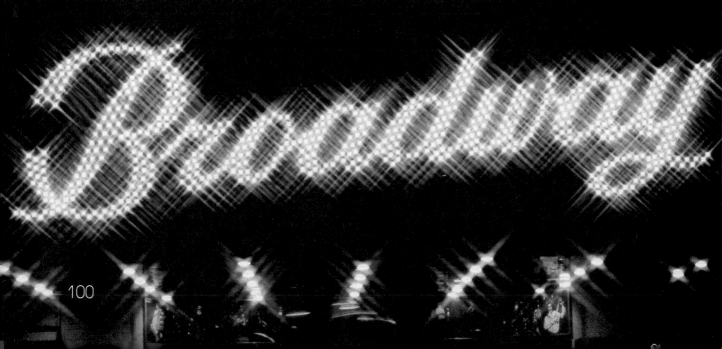

Making Heat and Light

The sun is not the only thing that gives us heat and light. **Fire** also gives us heat and light. Some people use fire for heat. Some people use fire for light. How is fire used in your home? How is fire being used in the pictures?

People use light bulbs for heat and light. Most light bulbs are used for light when it is dark. Some light bulbs are used just for heat. People use them to keep food warm. Can you think of other ways that light bulbs can be used?

A few things give off light without giving off heat. Have you ever seen a lightning bug? Why are they easy to see at night? Have you ever caught a lightning bug? Did it feel warm?

These things give off heat but not light. Why is it hard to tell when they are hot? What other things give off heat but not light?

Some things may not look hot. We cannot see heat. You should not touch things that might be hot.

How can you use energy from the sun?

- Put one ice cube in each cup.
- Put each cup in a box.
- Cover one box with clear plastic wrap.
- Cover one box with cardboard.

How are the two boxes different?

- Put the boxes in the sun.

What will happen to the ice cubes?

- Wait one-half hour.

How are the ice cubes different?

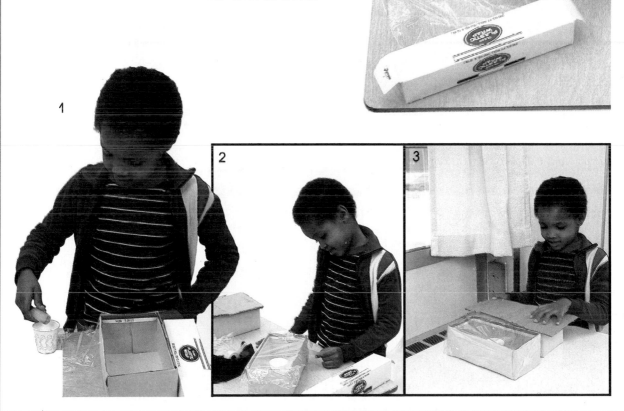

Reflecting Light

Many things do not give off their own light. Rocks, trees, and water do not give off their own light. Can you name other things that do not give off their own light? How do we see things that do not give off their own light? We need light to help us see these things.

We can see things that do not give off their own light. We can see them because they **reflect** light. Light bounces off things that reflect light. What is giving off light in each of the pictures? What is reflecting light in each of the pictures?

Look at the picture of the car under the bridge. There is very little light under the bridge. This makes the car hard to see.

Now look at the same car in the next picture. The car in the second picture is easier to see. One reason is that it is closer. What is another reason? The car reflects more light from the sun. What would you see if the picture was taken at night?

There is not much light at night.
Look at this picture. What things can
you see? Why can you see them? What
would you see if the picture were taken
during the day?

Good Reflectors

Some things reflect light better than other things. Light colors reflect light better than dark colors. Look at the picture. Who is easier to see? Do you know why?

Smooth, shiny things reflect much light. A mirror is smooth and reflects light well. How is the water in the picture like a mirror?

Some things that reflect light well are called **reflectors**. You might have seen some reflectors used on a highway. Do you have a reflector on your bicycle? In what other ways can people use reflectors?

 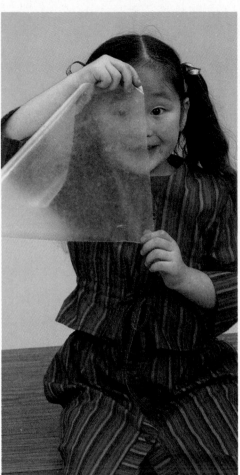 

Not all the light that shines on objects is reflected. Light passes through some things. Some things let only part of the light pass through. Some things do not let any light pass through. Look at the pictures. Which object lets the most light pass through?

Sometimes we do not want heat to move through things. The things shown in the pictures keep heat from moving. What other things can keep heat from moving?

Changing Heat Energy

Things with lots of heat energy are warm. Rubbing your hands together makes them warmer. You are adding heat energy. Putting your hands in ice water makes them cold. You are taking heat energy away. How can you make your hands warm again?

How can we tell if things are hot or cold? One way is to feel them. But some things are too hot to touch. We can use a **thermometer** to **measure** hot and cold.

How do you read a thermometer?

- Put a thermometer into ice water.
- Watch the color move.

Which way does it move?

- Read the numbers where it stops.

What do the numbers tell you?

- Put the thermometer into warm water.

Does the color move in the same way?

What is the temperature of the water?

Using Heat and Light

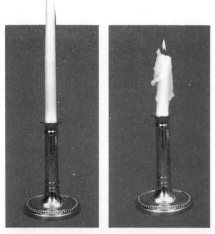

We use heat and light energy every day. We use heat energy to change things. Food changes when we cook it. How did the things in the pictures change? What do you think made each change?

We use heat in many ways. We use it to keep our homes warm. We use it to dry our clothes. In what other ways do we use heat energy?

Light energy is also very important. We use it to light our homes. We use it to light our streets. How have you used light energy today?

Check It Now

WORDS TO KNOW

Fill in the missing word in each sentence.

reflect   thermometer   heat   light   energy

1. Heat is a kind of _____.

2. We use a _____ to measure heat energy.

3. Shiny objects _____ more light than dull objects.

4. The sun gives us light, which changes to _____ energy.

5. We can see a candle because of _____ energy.

IDEAS TO KNOW

Which things give off both heat and light?

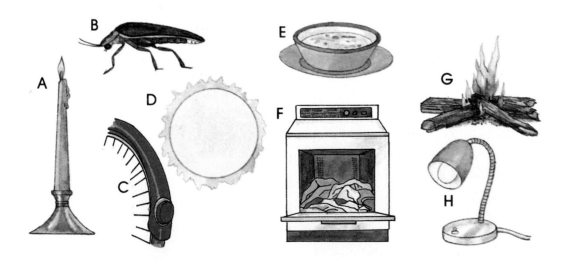

Choose the one in each pair that reflects light better.

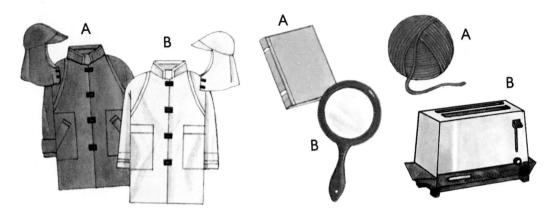

The thermometer outside looks like this.
How will you dress to go outside?

USING IDEAS

Why do police always warn trick or treaters
at Halloween to carry a flashlight?

Why should people who are outside at night
always wear light-colored clothes?

7

Our Earth's Air and Water

You know that you live on the **earth**. But do you know that much of the earth is covered with water? Do you know that the earth is also covered with a blanket of air? Plants and animals need air and water to live. Do you need air and water to live?

The Air Around You

Air is all around you. It covers the earth like a blanket. It is outdoors and indoors. Air is in large spaces and small spaces. Where can you find air in these pictures?

How do you know air is all around you? You cannot see air. It does not have color or a shape of its own. You cannot taste or smell air. But you do know that air is all around. You can feel air move. You can see it move things. You can hear it move things.

Moving air is called **wind**. How do you know that air is in the pictures? How do you know that air in the pictures is moving?

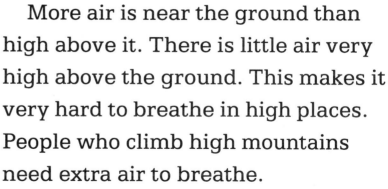

More air is near the ground than high above it. There is little air very high above the ground. This makes it very hard to breathe in high places. People who climb high mountains need extra air to breathe.

There is also air in the soil. Some things live in the soil. They need the air that is there. This worm moves through the soil. How does it help let air into the soil?

How can we tell if air is in the jar?

- Put a plastic bag over a jar.
- Use a rubber band to hold the bag tightly.
- Try to push the bag all the way into the jar.

Does the bag go into the jar?

What is in the jar?

- Remove the rubber band.
- Push part of the bag inside the jar.
- Put the rubber band tightly around the jar.
- Try to pull the bag out of the jar.

Can you pull the bag all the way out? Why?

127

Air in Water

Air is also in water. Fish live in water. They need air to live. Fish get air from the water by using their **gills.** Water plants use the air in water also. Look at the fish in the picture below. Why do people add air to fish tanks?

People cannot get air from water. How do you think the swimmer in the picture breathes underwater?

How can we tell that there is air in water?

- Fill a clean glass with water.
- Place a metal spoon in the glass.
- Leave the spoon there until the next day.
- Do not move the spoon at all.
- Look in the glass.

What do you see?

- Use a hand lens to take a closer look.

What would happen if you moved the glass?

Water on the Earth

Look at the picture of the earth. Most of the earth is covered by water. You can see that most of the water is in oceans. But water is also in lakes, ponds, and rivers. This water is **fresh water**. It is not the same as ocean water. Ocean water is salty. People call it **salt water**. Salt water is not good to drink.

Activity

How does an object float in salt water and in fresh water?

- Put the same amount of cold water into two cups.
- Mix three spoons of salt into one cup.
- Put a small ball of clay in one end of a straw.
- Hold the straw down in one cup and let it go.
- On the side of the cup, mark where the straw stops.
- Do the same thing with the other cup.

How are the marks different?

Where Do We Find Water?

Many people do not live near lakes and rivers. Where do they get their water? They get it from the ground. **Wells** are dug to find water deep in the ground. Water is then pumped to the top of the well.

Sometimes people build lakes to collect rainwater and melted snow. Large amounts of water are stored in these lakes. The water is then used in homes and factories. These lakes are called **reservoirs**.

Have you ever seen puddles dry up? Where do you think the water goes? Most of the water goes into the ground. And some of it goes into the air. You cannot see most of the water in the air. But you can see water in the air when it forms clouds.

Sometimes the water leaves the clouds. It falls back to the earth as rain, snow, and sleet. Look at the pictures. Where did the water go?

Frozen Water

Some places on the earth are very cold. The water in these cold places is always frozen. Water that **freezes** is called **ice**. Do you think there is ice in this place all year?

In other places water freezes only in the winter. Ice covers rivers, ponds, and lakes. Is there ice where you live in the winter? What happens to the ice in the spring?

Look at the pictures. The water in one picture is frozen. Ice floats on water. This is because it weighs less than water. What do you think happens to living things in a frozen pond?

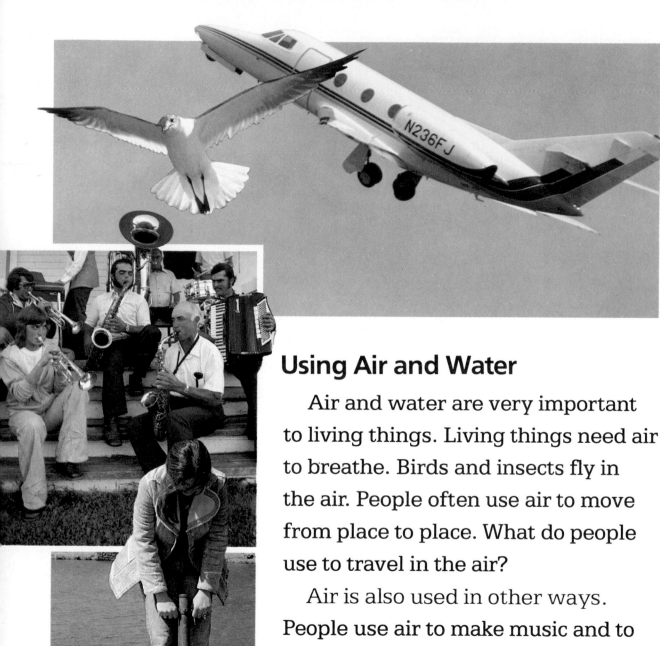

Using Air and Water

Air and water are very important to living things. Living things need air to breathe. Birds and insects fly in the air. People often use air to move from place to place. What do people use to travel in the air?

Air is also used in other ways. People use air to make music and to dry things. Air helps you hear sounds. Air is also used for filling balls and other things. How is air being used in these pictures?

Living things need water to live. People use water to cook and clean. They even use water to have fun. People use boats to move things from place to place on water. Can you think of other ways people use water? In which picture are both air and water being used?

Dirty Air and Water

We should take care of our air and water. Dirty air is called **polluted** air. Cars, trucks, and airplanes can make air dirty. Factories can also make air dirty.

Polluted air is harmful to plants and animals. It can also make people sick. What can we do to keep the air clean?

Clean water can be used for having fun. The people in the picture above are enjoying clean water.

Dirty water is called polluted water. Polluted water is harmful to all living things. It can kill fish. It can harm people who drink it. It cannot be used for cooking. And it cannot be used for having fun. Some factories put waste in the water. Sometimes people dump trash in it. What can we do to keep water clean?

Check It Now

WORDS TO KNOW

Solve the riddles, using the words in the box.

salt water   gills   ice   reservoir   air

1. I am all around you, but I cannot be seen.
2. I store water for homes and factories.
3. When I am around, you can walk on pond water.
4. Objects float higher in me.
5. Fish use me to get air from the water.

IDEAS TO KNOW

There are five science mistakes in this story.
Read the story and find each mistake.

   Kathy and her dad went down to the beach.
"I just love the ocean," said her Dad. "It is
too bad that most of the earth is covered by land."

   "That fresh ocean water feels good on my skin,"
said Kathy. "I'm so thirsty, I think I'll have
a drink of it."

As she bent down to get a drink, Kathy saw a fish. "Look!" she said. "I see a fish using its gills to paddle through the water. It has not come up for air. I guess fish do not need air to live, because they live in water."

IDEAS TO KNOW

Which pictures show air being used?
Which pictures show water being used?
Which pictures show both air and water being used?

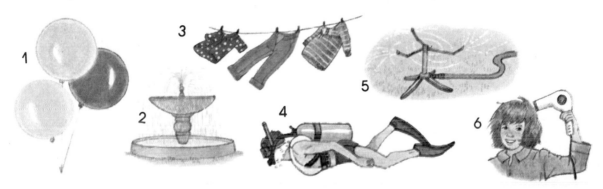

USING IDEAS

Andy brought a starfish home from the beach. He wanted it for a pet. He put it in a tank with fresh water. It did not live long. Why should Andy have left the starfish in its ocean home?

8

Our Sun

There are many stars in the night sky. On a clear night you can see thousands of them. Do you know that these stars are like the sun? The **sun** is a very hot star. It is the star closest to the earth. It is the only star we can see in the daytime sky. The sun is very important to us.

What Is the Sun Like?

The sun is shaped like a giant ball. It is much larger than the earth. Let's suppose the sun were the size of a basketball. How big do you think the earth would be? The earth would be as big as the head of a pin. More than a million earths could fit into the sun.

The earth gets light from the sun. When **sunlight** strikes the earth, the light changes to heat. In the winter less light strikes the earth. That is why winter is colder than summer.

Some places on the earth get more sunlight than others. Places near the middle of the earth get more sunlight. Places near the North Pole and the South Pole get less sunlight. Look at the pictures. Is it hot or cold in these places?

Night and Day

In the morning the sun seems to rise in the east. It seems to move across the sky during the day. At noontime it is high in the sky. In the evening it seems to set in the west.

We get the most sunlight during the day. Because of this we get the most heat during the day. At night we do not get sunlight. Is it as warm at

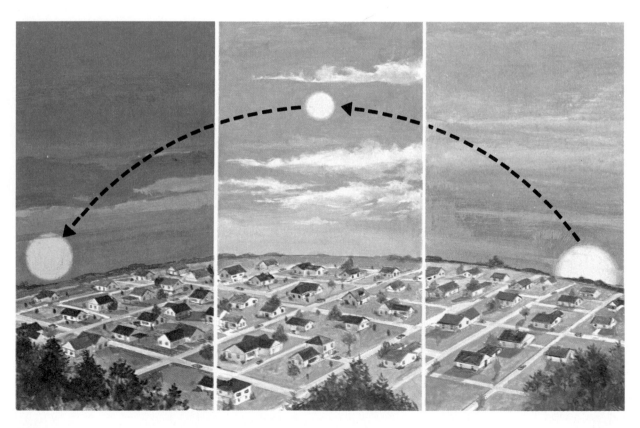

night as it is during the day? When does it begin to get warmer?

A **globe** is shaped like the earth. The earth and a globe are both round like a ball. The earth and a globe both turn. A globe can be used to show how the sun rises and sets. The children are looking at a globe to find where they live.

The Turning Earth

These children put a globe in a dark room. They marked the place where they live with a piece of tape. Now they are shining a flashlight on the globe. They are pretending that the light is the sun.

Where will the tape be if they turn the globe halfway around? Will the light still be shining on the tape? The place with the tape becomes dark as the globe turns away from the sun.

The light shines on only one half of the globe. It does not shine on the other half at the same time.

This is what happens on the earth. The sun shines on only half of the earth at any time. It is daytime on this half of the earth. People on the other half of the earth do not see the sun. It is nighttime there. The sun does not move. The turning earth causes night to change to day.

The earth is always turning. It never stops turning. You cannot see or feel it turning. It makes one complete turn every day. How many times does the earth turn in a week?

How does the earth turn each day?

- Stand and face a lamp.

Where does the light shine on you?

- Slowly turn around in the same place.

How are you like the earth?

Where is the sun?

Your face moves in and out of the light.

What is this like?

Using Shadows to Tell Time

Some people use the sun to tell time. They look to see where the sun is in the sky. They know the sun is first seen in the east. It is early when the sun is low in the east. What time is it if the sun is overhead in the sky? It is late in the day when the sun sets in the west.

Long ago, people did not have clocks to tell time. They used a sundial. The sun made a **shadow** on the sundial. People used the shadow to tell time.

Shadows are longer when the sun is lower in the sky. What is your shadow like at noontime? You can see how shadows can be helpful for telling time. How has the shadow on the sundial in the pictures changed? Is a sundial helpful on cloudy days?

How do shadows change during the day?

- Go outside on a sunny morning.
- Have a partner trace your shadow with a piece of chalk.
- Do this again near lunchtime and in the afternoon.
- Be sure you are standing in the same place.

How has your shadow changed since morning?

Some things make bigger shadows than others. The size of any shadow depends on two things. It depends on the time of day. It also depends on the size of an object. Things that are big have big shadows. Small things have small shadows. Suppose you wanted to sit in the shade. Would you sit near a flagpole or under a large tree?

Using Sunlight

Green plants use sunlight to make food. They need the food they make to grow. Many plants grow parts that we use for food. We eat leaves, stems, and fruits of plants. What other parts of plants do we eat?

Animals also eat plants. A cow eats grass. The cow uses the grass to make milk. We drink the milk. How does the sun help give us milk to drink?

Sunlight that strikes the earth is changed to heat. Heat from sunlight is very important to us. What would happen if sunlight did not change to heat? Some people use sunlight to heat their homes. Some people even cook with the heat from sunlight.

Scientists are always trying to find new uses for the sun's energy. They have found ways to use sunlight to run motors. Special panels are used on space capsules to collect sunlight. The sunlight is changed to electricity.

The sun is important to us. But it can be harmful, too. Never look right at the sun. The light can hurt your eyes. Spending too much time in the sun can also be harmful. Sunlight can burn your skin. Sunburn can be very painful. You should use suntan lotion when you are in the sun for a long time. Can you think of other ways the sun can be harmful?

Check It Now

WORDS TO KNOW

Use the letters to make words that tell about the sun.

Use each word in a sentence.

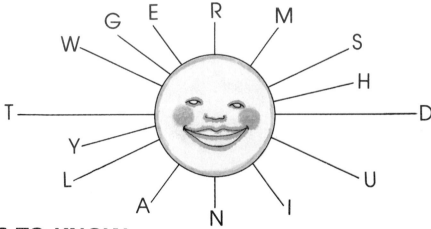

IDEAS TO KNOW

Which pictures show how the sun is harmful?

Which pictures show how the sun is helpful?

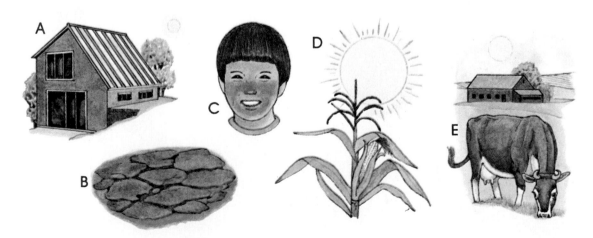

Match the sentences with the pictures.

1. Many plants need energy from the sun to grow.
2. This is our closest star.
3. This is a clock that uses shadows.
4. This is a model of the earth.
5. It is night when half of the earth is not facing the sun.

THINKING LIKE A SCIENTIST

1. Why can we think of night as a moving shadow?
2. Imagine that you are lost. You need to travel north. How could a watch and shadows help you to find your way?

9

Our Weather

Changes in the air around the earth are called the weather. Clouds and wind help tell us about the weather. The weather changes from day to day and from season to season. What can you tell about the weather in the pictures?

Temperature

The temperature of the air helps tell us about the weather. **Temperature** tells us how hot or cold something is. We use a thermometer to measure temperature. The liquid in the thermometer goes up when the air gets warm. The liquid goes down when the air gets cold.

Reading the temperature on a thermometer helps us know what clothes to wear. Can you read the temperature on a thermometer? Can you tell when the air is warm or cold?

The pictures show four different places. The temperature in each place is different. Some places stay warm all year. Some places stay cold most of the year. In other places the temperature changes. What is the temperature like in each place? What would you wear in each place?

Clouds

Clouds are made up of tiny drops of water or ice. Some clouds are high in the sky. **Fog** is a cloud near the ground. There are many kinds of clouds with different shapes. The different kinds of clouds help tell us what the weather will be. What kinds of clouds are in the sky today? What will the weather be today?

You may see white fluffy clouds on a sunny day. The weather is usually fair on those days. Sometimes the weather is cloudy for a long time.

Some clouds can be very thick and dark. These clouds show us that the weather is changing. These clouds may bring rain or snow. They may bring a **storm**. Have you ever seen clouds like these? What was the weather like?

Some places have very dry air. One picture shows such a place. You do not see many clouds here. Very little rain falls here. Would you see many plants growing in a place like this?

The other picture shows a place where it rains every day. It is very warm in this place. Many plants grow here. Do you know why there are so many plants?

How do clouds help you tell about the weather?

- Use cotton to make pictures of clouds.
- Make some fair-weather clouds.
- Make some storm clouds.

Tell about these clouds.

How are storm clouds and
fair-weather clouds different?

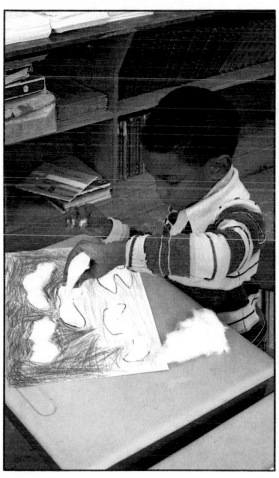

Wind

Wind is moving air. The wind changes when the weather changes. It can bring clouds and rain. It can also take away clouds.

Sometimes the wind can be helpful. Sometimes it can be fun. The wind can also be harmful. The wind blows very hard during storms.

Sometimes the wind blows hard. At other times the wind blows gently. The wind is always changing. Sudden strong winds are called **gusts**. Gentle winds are called **breezes**. If the wind does not blow, the weather is calm.

You know that wind is moving air. What can you tell about the wind by looking outside? The wind makes things move. You can see them move. Which picture shows a gust of wind? Which shows a gentle breeze? Which picture shows calm weather?

We use these things to measure the wind. One shows how fast the wind is blowing. The other shows which way the wind is blowing. It points in the direction the wind is coming from. We call this one a **wind vane**.

Look at the picture of the wind vane. From which direction is the wind blowing? Wind from the west is called west wind. What would wind from the north be called?

How does the wind help living things?

- Take a walk outside.
- Find some things that the wind moves.
- Find some things that the wind helps.
- Find some things that the wind may harm.

What does the wind do?

Harmful Weather

Some weather can be very harmful. Strong winds can blow trees down. Winds can blow the roofs off houses. Some winds can even destroy buildings. Heavy snowstorms can stop cars and trucks. How else do you think weather can be harmful?

Water flows into streams and rivers when it rains. Too much rain can cause **floods**. This picture shows a flood. Floods happen when rivers and streams cannot hold all the water. Then the water flows over the land. Melting snow can also cause floods. At what time of year would this happen?

Floods can cause a lot of damage. What happens to plants and animals when there are floods?

Why Weather Is Important

Weather is important to people. It can be important to the work they do. Weather is important to the farmer. Sunshine helps plants to grow. Rain is also needed to help plants grow.

Weather is important to a mail carrier. Mail carriers work outdoors. Sometimes weather makes their job difficult. How is the weather important to other workers?

Weather is important for the things you do for fun. On sunny summer days you can swim and play outdoors. In the winter some people have fun in the snow. Many people like to ski and to go sledding. Some people like to skate on frozen ponds. What do you do for fun in the winter?

Changes Made by Weather

Animals change with the weather. The pictures above show the same rabbit. The rabbit has changed. How does this change help the rabbit? The horses in the picture have grown thick coats. Their coats will help keep them warm.

You change the kind of clothing you wear when the weather changes, too. Why do you change your clothing when winter comes?

What can you tell about the weather by looking at a weather chart?

- Make a chart like this.
- Write the name of this month on the line.
- Draw pictures that show the weather.

How many days this month were sunny?

What was the weather like most of the time?

	Monday	Tuesday	Wednesday	Thursday	Friday
JANUARY					
First Week					
Second Week					
Third week					
Fourth week					

WORDS TO KNOW

Read the weather report. Fill in the missing words.

clouds   rain   calm   temperature   floods

The _____ which caused the terrible _____ has
ended. The high _____ today will be 50 degrees.
The wind is _____ and from the north. There
are fair weather _____ in the sky.

IDEAS TO KNOW

Match the thermometers with the weather pictures.

180

What kinds of weather do these clouds bring? Use these words. Fair Stormy Changing

A
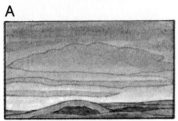

B

C

Tell how the weather is helpful or harmful.

A

B

C

D

THINKING LIKE A SCIENTIST

Water can change from a liquid to a gas.

Clouds form when water changes back to a liquid.

Clouds are made of tiny drops of water or ice.

●Blow on a mirror.

What happens?

How is blowing on a mirror like clouds forming in the sky?

10

Keeping Safe

Learning about safety will help you stay healthy. There are **safety rules** for home and school. What safety rules do you know? How are the people in the pictures following safety rules?

Home Safety

Fire can be helpful. Can you name ways it is helpful? But fire can also be harmful. You should never play with matches. Playing with matches can cause house fires.

You should know what to do in case of a fire at home. Practice a home fire drill with your family. Does your family have a special place outdoors to meet in case of a fire? Do you know how to use the telephone to call for help? Talk to your family about fire safety in your home.

There are many things for you to know about fire safety. What campfire rules can you name? What other fire safety rules can you name?

Some things in your home can hurt you. Many things used for cleaning or gardening can harm your body. They can harm your skin and eyes. You should not breathe these things. You should never put them into your mouth.

Look for danger signs on the labels of bottles, cans, and boxes. Look for the words DANGER, CAUTION, POISON, or WARNING. These words mean that you need to be careful.

Tools in your home can also hurt you. Always ask an adult to help you use tools.

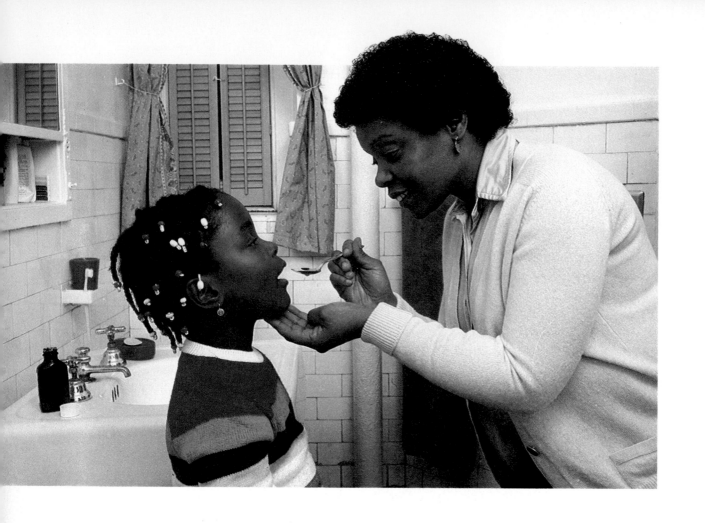

Some people have to take **medicine** when they are sick. Medicine can help you feel better. You should only take medicine from an adult. You should never take any medicine that belongs to someone else. Taking it can make you sick. And taking too much medicine can also be harmful.

Medicines can sometimes look like candy. If you eat these medicines, you might become sick. Medicines have a label to help you. The label tells what the medicine is and how to use it. Medicines can be helpful. But they can also be harmful.

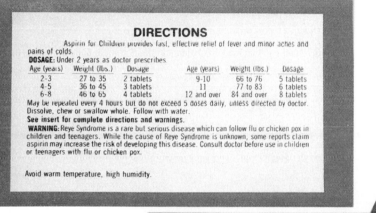

DIRECTIONS

Aspirin for Children provides fast, effective relief of fever and minor aches and pains of colds.

DOSAGE: Under 2 years as doctor prescribes.

Age (years)	Weight (lbs.)	Dosage	Age (years)	Weight (lbs.)	Dosage
2-3	27 to 35	2 tablets	9-10	66 to 76	5 tablets
4-5	36 to 45	3 tablets	11	77 to 83	6 tablets
6-8	46 to 65	4 tablets	12 and over	84 and over	8 tablets

May be repeated every 4 hours but do not exceed 5 doses daily, unless directed by doctor. Dissolve, chew or swallow whole. Follow with water.

See insert for complete directions and warnings.

WARNING: Reye Syndrome is a rare but serious disease which can follow flu or chicken pox in children and teenagers. While the cause of Reye Syndrome is unknown, some reports claim aspirin may increase the risk of developing this disease. Consult doctor before use in children or teenagers with flu or chicken pox.

Avoid warm temperature, high humidity.

Bicycle Safety

Safety is important when riding a bicycle. Safety starts with making sure your bicycle is safe. Look at the bicycles in the pictures. Can you find reflectors? What other things make these bicycles safe?

Choosing the right bicycle will help you ride safely. A bicycle that is too big is unsafe to ride. There is a way to tell if a bicycle is the right size for you. Sit on the seat. Try to touch the ground with your feet. The bicycle is too big if your feet do not touch the ground. Which bicycle in the pictures is safe for the rider?

When riding a bicycle, sometimes you share the street with cars and trucks. You must also obey the same rules as drivers of cars and trucks. You should stop at stop signs and red lights. What other rules should bicycle riders obey?

You should ride your bicycle close to the right side of the street. Riding single file is a good rule to follow.

You should also know hand signals.
Look at the pictures. Do the hand
signals tell you what the rider is
going to do? What do they tell you?

Why should you wear light-colored clothing at night?

- Draw two shapes.
- Make one shape brown.
- Make the other white.
- Cut the shapes out.
- Paste them side by side on black paper.
- Turn out the lights in the room.

Which shape is easier to see?

Traveling Safely

Safety is important when riding in a car. A seat belt can protect you from being injured. It keeps you in your seat in case of an accident. Be sure to put your seat belt on before the car moves. Be a safety helper. Make sure other people in the car also wear seat belts. Younger children should use a car seat. Be sure to leave your seat belt on until the car stops.

Some accidents happen when people get into or out of a parked car. Be sure you get into and out of a car on the curb side. Using this side keeps you away from traffic in the street.

How do seat belts help us?

- Tightly strap an egg into a toy car.
- Use a board to make a road.
- Hold the car at the top of the road.

What will happen when you let go?

- Let the car go down the road.

What happened?

- Take off the "seat belt."

What will happen this time?

- Let the car go.

Why are seat belts important?

Do you ride a bus or walk to school? Bus safety is important for all children. Many children ride a bus to school. Safety starts before you get on the bus. Stand back from the curb. Why is it important not to push others in line? Do not run to the bus. Find a seat and sit down before the bus moves. Talk quietly to friends on the bus. Why is a noisy bus unsafe?

Stay seated until the bus stops for you to get off. What might happen if the bus moves while you are standing?

Walk carefully down the steps of the bus. Walk ten steps away from the bus. If you must cross the street, look to see that all traffic has stopped. Then cross. Walk carefully in front of the bus.

Do you walk to school? You may pass a school bus on the way. You may walk near buses parked at school. Bus safety is important for all children. Why are these safety rules important? Never walk behind a parked bus. Do not walk between parked buses.

Why is it dangerous to walk close to a bus?

- Look at the driver on the bus.

Whom can the driver see?

Where is it safe for children to walk?

What should you do if you drop something
near the bus?

- Practice bus safety on a bus at
  your school.

- Get on and off the bus safely.

- Show how to act at the bus stop.

What are some good bus
safety rules?

Playing Safely

Some places are made for playing and having fun. Parks and playgrounds are safe places for having fun. But you also should be careful when playing in these places. There is a safe way to use the things in the playground. Playing in the playground in the wrong way is unsafe. Look at the pictures. How are the children using these things safely?

Playing safely also means following the rules in any game you play. Learn the skills for each game. Also learn to use bats, balls, and other things for sports. Always remember to take turns and to be thoughtful. Playing safely and fairly makes playing more fun for everyone.

Do you know how to swim? Swimming and playing in water can be fun. Safety rules are important when you are near water. A good rule is never to swim alone. Always swim with a friend. Swimming with a friend is safer. It is also more fun. Always be sure an adult is watching you when you are swimming.

Playing with friends is fun. Friends like to wait for the bus together. They like to walk to school together. Talking with friends is fun, too. These things are fun to do and safe.

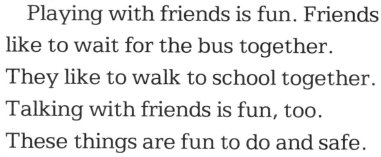

Talking to strangers is not safe. Walking with people we do not know is not safe. Suppose a stranger tells you he is lost. Should you show him the way to go? Suppose someone wants to give you a ride. She says your mother needs you. What should you do?

What if a stranger wants to give you
a present? Everyone likes to get
presents. Why shouldn't you take
things from people you do not know?
What can you do if a stranger wants
to give you a present?

Have you ever been lost? Sometimes
you need to ask others for help. Whom
can you talk to when you are lost?

Check It Now

WORDS TO KNOW

Complete the safety rules. Use these words.

swim   seat belt   bicycle   poison

1. For safety, check your _____.
2. _____ can hurt you.
3. Always _____ with a friend.
4. Buckle your _____.

IDEAS TO KNOW

Look at the pictures. Which pictures show children following safety rules?

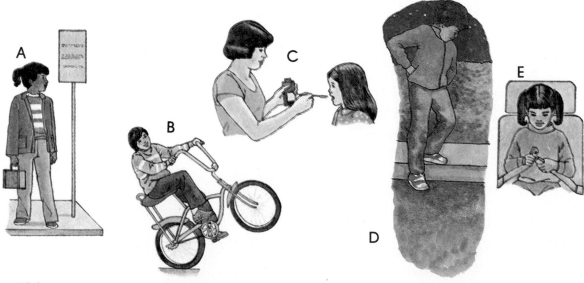

A

B

C

D

E

206

IDEAS TO KNOW

Draw a picture to show each safety rule.

1. Look for danger signs.
2. Learn what to do in case of a fire.
3. Never go with a stranger.

What things make a bicycle safe? Use these words to name them.

reflector   flag   light   horn   brakes

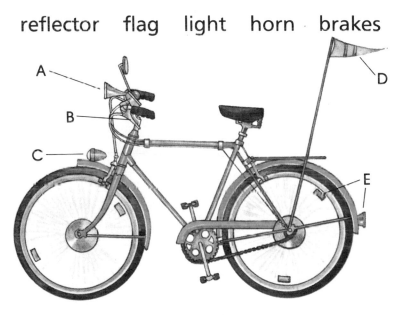

USING IDEAS

Why do many signs have pictures rather than words to warn people?

What do you think each of these signs means?

Science in Careers

People use science at home and in their work. Science helps them ask questions. Science helps them find the answers. Science helps people in their jobs.

Teachers use science. They help children learn about the world.

Builders use science. They build houses. They build skyscrapers. They build bridges. They build all kinds of things.

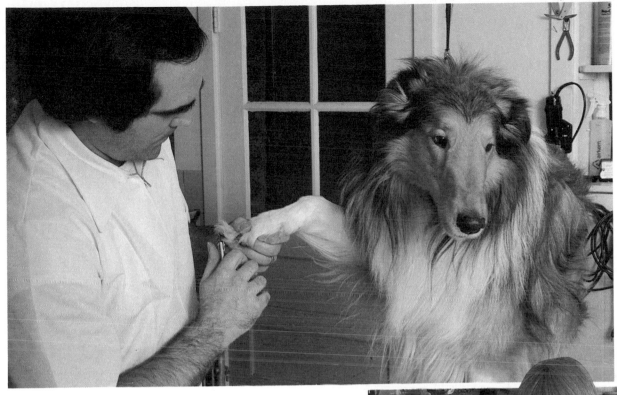

Animal doctors use science. They help to keep animals healthy.

People who work with plants use science. Gardeners grow plants and take care of them. Florists sell plants.

Science Words

A

air   The layer of gases that is all around the earth. We breathe air. (page 74)

attract   To pull to or toward. A magnet will attract a paper clip. (page 84)

B

breeze   A gentle wind. The breeze is making the flag move. (page 171)

C

clouds   A large mass of tiny drops of water or ice floating in the air. (page 166)

D

desert   A place where very little rain falls. The desert is dry and sandy. (page 50)

dinosaur   An animal that lived long ago. (page 1)

E

earth   The planet where we live. (page 122)

electricity   A kind of energy used to make heat and light. Electricity makes a lamp light. (page 158)

endangered   In danger of dying out. Leopards are endangered animals. (page 18)

energy   The power to do work. Heat, light, and electricity are different kinds of energy. (page 100)

F

fall   The season of the year that comes before winter. Plants die or rest in the fall. (page 35)

fire   Flame, heat, and light given off when something burns. (page 102)

flood   Water that flows out over land. Many days of rain may cause a flood. (page 175)

flower   The part of a plant in which the seed forms. (page 29)

fog   A cloud close to the ground. (page 166)

footprint   A mark made by a foot. Dinosaurs made footprints in the mud. (page 4)

freeze   To change into a solid because of cold. Water becomes ice when it freezes. (page 134)

fresh water   Water that is not salty. We can drink fresh water. (page 130)

fruit   The part of a plant where seeds are found. An apple is a fruit. (page 30)

G

gas Matter that has no shape or size of its own. Air is made up of gases. (page 74)

gill The part of the body that a fish uses to get air from the water. (page 128)

globe A round ball with a map of the world on it. (page 147)

grow To become bigger. People, animals, and plants grow. (page 22)

gust A sudden strong wind. A gust of wind made the kites fly higher. (page 171)

H

heat A kind of energy. The heat from the fire makes us warm. (page 100)

I

ice Water that is frozen. The pond is covered with ice. (page 134)

L

leaves Thin, flat green parts of a plant. (page 27)

light A kind of energy we can see. The sun gives light energy to the earth. (page 100)

liquid Matter that changes shape when it is poured. Water is a liquid. (page 73)

M

magnet   A stone or piece of metal that attracts some other metals. Some magnets are made by people. (page 82)

matter   Anything that takes up space and has weight. Matter can be a solid, a liquid, or a gas. (page 66)

measure   To find how much there is of something. You can measure temperature with a thermometer. (page 116)

medicine   Something used to help sick people and animals to get well. (page 190)

O

ocean   A large body of salt water. Oceans cover most of the earth's surface. (page 56)

P

plants   Living things that are not animals. Many plants have roots, stems, and leaves. (page 22)

poles   The ends of a magnet. A magnet is strongest at the poles. (page 88)

pollute   To make air and water dirty. Smoke from factories pollutes the air. (page 138)

pond A small lake. Many plants and animals live in a pond. (page 54)

R

reflect To throw back. Shiny things reflect light. (page 107)

reflector Something that reflects light well. A mirror is a good reflector. (page 111)

repel To push away. Poles of two magnets that are alike repel. (page 92)

reservoir A lake where water is stored for use in homes and factories. (page 132)

root The part of a plant that grows down into the soil. (page 27)

S

salt water Water that has salt in it. Ocean water is salt water. (page 130)

scientist Someone who studies science. A scientist tries to find answers to questions about science. (page 158)

season One of the four parts of a year. Spring, summer, fall, and winter are seasons. (page 32)

seed The part of a plant that can grow a new plant. We planted an apple seed. (page 24)

seed coat   The cover around a seed. (page 26)

shadow   A dark shape made when light is blocked by a person or thing. We make shadows on the ground on sunny days. (page 153)

skull   The bone found in the head of an animal. The skull holds and protects the brain. (page 14)

solid   Matter that has a shape of its own. A rock is a solid. (page 72)

space capsule   The front part of a rocket used to carry people and things into space. (page 158)

spring   The season after winter when plants begin to grow. (page 33)

star   An object that looks like a point of light in the sky at night. Stars give off light. (page 142)

stem   The main part of a plant that holds the leaves and flowers. (page 27)

storm   A strong wind with rain, snow, or hail. People stay indoors during a bad storm. (page 167)

summer   The warmest season of the year. The days are longer in the summer. (page 34)

sun   The brightest object in the daytime sky. The earth gets light and heat from the sun. (page 142)

swamp Land where the ground is wet all of the time. (page 6)

T

temperature The measure of heat in an object. (page 164)

thermometer An instrument that measures the heat in an object. (page 116)

W

weather Changes in the air around the earth. Some people like rainy weather. (page 162)

weight The measure of how heavy something is. (page 68)

well A hole dug to reach water under the ground. (page 132)

wind Moving air. (page 170)

wind vane An object that shows the direction that the wind is coming from. (page 172)

winter Winter is the coldest of the four seasons. Days are short in the winter. (page 35)

woods A place where many trees and flowers grow. (page 42)

Index

Credits

Cover: Michael Adams

Other art: John Dawson, Leigh Grant, Rebecca Merrilees, Taylor Oughton, Ed Valigursky

The Adventure of Science   A–B: Mark Newman/Tom Stack & Associates; A: *r.* Andrew Odum/Peter Arnold, Inc. B: *t.l.* E.R. Degginger; *b.l.* Minneapolis Aquatennial Society; *m.r.* E.R. Degginger. C: Dan De Wilde for Silver Burdett & Ginn. D: *l.* © Richard Hutchings/Photo Researchers, Inc.; *t.r.* Dan De Wilde for Silver Burdett & Ginn; *b.r.* Imagery for Silver Burdett & Ginn. E: Dan De Wilde for Silver Burdett & Ginn.

Chapter 1   vi: *b.l.* Jane Burton, Steve Kirk/Bruce Coleman. vi–1: Jane Burton/Bruce Coleman. 2: Phil Degginger. 3: Norman Tomalin/Bruce Coleman. 4: *l.* Norman Myers/Bruce Coleman; *t.r., m.r.* E.R. Degginger. 5: Victoria Beller-Smith for Silver Burdett & Ginn. 14: Victoria Beller-Smith for Silver Burdett & Ginn. 18: *t.l.* Steven Kaufman/Peter Arnold, Inc; *b.l.* Bob and Clara Calhoun/Bruce Coleman; *t.r.* Fred Bavendam/Peter Arnold, Inc.; *m.r.* E.R. Degginger; *b.r.* John MacGregor/Peter Arnold, Inc. 19: *t.l.* George Harrison/Grant Heilman Photography; *b.l., t.r., b.r.* E.R. Degginger; *t.m.* E.R. Degginger/Bruce Coleman.

Chapter 2   22–23: Walter Chandoha. 24: *t.* Phil Degginger; *inset* © Leonard Lee Rue/Photo Researchers, Inc.; *m.r.* Walter Chandoha; *b.m., b.r.* Silver Burdett & Ginn. 25: *t.l.* Bruce Coleman; *b.l.* Grant Heilman Photography; *t.r.* Silver Burdett & Ginn; *b.r.* Fukuhara Photography/West Light. 26: Silver Burdett & Ginn. 29: *t.r.* Lynn Bodek; *b.* © Russ Kinne/Photo Researchers, Inc. 30: *t.l., t.r.* E.R. Degginger; *m.l.* W.H. Hodge/Peter Arnold, Inc. 31: Dan De Wilde for Silver Burdett & Ginn. 32: Clyde Smith/Peter Arnold, Inc. 35: *t.l.* © Charles Beliky/Photo Researchers, Inc.; *m.l.* Walter Chandoha; *t.r.* Imagery. 36–37: Silver Burdett & Ginn.

Chapter 3   40: *b.l.* E.R. Degginger; *r.* © Lowell Georgia/Photo Researchers, Inc. 40–41: *b.r., t.r.* Ed Rescher/Peter Arnold, Inc. 41: *t.l.* Bill Gillette/Stock, Boston. 43–44: E.R. Degginger. 45: *l.* E.R. Degginger; *t.l.inset* © Bill Dyer/Photo Researchers, Inc.; *t.l.* E.R. Degginger; *b.r. inset* Breck Kent. 46: *l., t.l. inset* E.R. Degginger; *r., r. inset* © Harald Sund. 47: Stephen Krasemann/Peter Arnold, Inc.; *inset* Lynn Bodek. 48: *t.l.* E.R. Degginger; *t.r.* Jane Burton/Bruce Coleman. 49: Dan De Wilde for Silver Burdett & Ginn. 50: Alan Pitcairn/Grant Heilman Photography. 51: *t.l.* © Harald Sund; *m.l.* E.R. Degginger; *t.r.* C. Allan Morgan/Peter Arnold, Inc.; *m.r.* John Gerlach/Tom Stack & Associates. 52: E.R. Degginger. 53: Silver Burdett & Ginn. 56: *t.* NASA; *inset* Silver Burdett & Ginn. 57: Silver Burdett & Ginn. 58: *t.l.* E.R. Degginger; *b.* Jane Shaw/Bruce Coleman. 59: *t., m.l.* Fred Bavendam/Peter Arnold, Inc.; *m.r.* E.R. Degginger.

Chapter 4   62: *b.l.* Lincoln Russell/Stock, Boston; *t.r.* © Susan McCartney/Photo Researchers, Inc. 62–63: Grant Heilman Photography. 63: *t.l.* © Dr. Gregory Dimijian/Photo Researchers, Inc.; *r.* Richard A. Blake/Click/Chicago. 64: *t.l.* © Elizabeth Weiland/Photo Researchers, Inc.; *m.* Walter Chandoha; *b.l.* Davis DeWitt/Artoz Images, Inc.; *b.r. inset* © Nelson Medina/Photo Researchers, Inc. 65: *t.l.* © Russ Kinne/Photo Researchers, Inc.; *t.m.* © Michael Philip Manheim/Photo Researchers, Inc.; *t.r.* © Allen Green/Photo Researchers, Inc.; *b.r.* © Richard Hutchings/Photo Researchers, Inc. 66: Silver Burdett & Ginn. 67: Dan De Wilde for Silver Burdett & Ginn. 68–70: Silver Burdett & Ginn. 71: Dan De Wilde for Silver Burdett & Ginn. 72–73: Silver Burdett & Ginn. 74: E.R. Degginger. 75–76: Silver Burdett & Ginn. 77: E.R. Degginger; *b.l. inset* E.R. Degginger; *t.r. inset* Silver Burdett & Ginn. 78: Stephen Krasemann/Peter Arnold, Inc. 79: Dan De Wilde for Silver Burdett & Ginn.

Chapter 5   82–84: Silver Burdett & Ginn. 85: Dan De Wilde for Silver Burdett & Ginn. 86–90: Silver Burdett & Ginn. 91: Dan De Wilde for Silver Burdett & Ginn. 92–93: Silver Burdett & Ginn. 94–95: Dan De Wilde for Silver Burdett & Ginn. 96: Silver Burdett & Ginn. 96–97: E.R. Degginger. 97: *t.r. inset* Silver Burdett & Ginn.

Chapter 6 100: *b.* Richard Laird/Leo deWys, Inc.; *t.r.* E.R. Degginger. 100–101: C.A. Morgan/Peter Arnold, Inc. 102: *t.l.* Breck Kent; *b.l.* Silver Burdett & Ginn; *b.r.* Keith Gunnar/Bruce Coleman. 103: *t.l.* Norman Thompson/ Taurus Photos; *t.r.* Silver Burdett & Ginn; *b.r.* E.R. Degginger. 104: *t.l.* Hickson-Bender for Silver Burdett & Ginn; *m.* Silver Burdett & Ginn. *b.l.* Dan De Wilde for Silver Burdett & Ginn. 105: Silver Burdett & Ginn. 106: E.R. Degginger. 107: *l.* Silver Burdett & Ginn; *r.* Victoria Beller-Smith for Silver Burdett & Ginn. 108: Silver Burdett & Ginn. 109: E.R. Degginger. 110: Bob Evans/Peter Arnold, Inc. 111: *t.* E.R. Degginger; *b.* Victoria Beller-Smith for Silver Burdett & Ginn. 112: Silver Burdett & Ginn. 113: Dan De Wilde for Silver Burdett & Ginn. 114: *t.* E.R. Degginger; *b.* Silver Burdett & Ginn. 115: *t.r., b.r.* Silver Burdett & Ginn; *l.* Beth Ullman/Taurus Photos. 116–118: Silver Burdett & Ginn. 119: *t.* Tom Stack & Associates; *b.* E.R. Degginger.

Chapter 7 122: *t.* Nicholas de Vore III/Bruce Coleman; *m.* Imagery; *b.* Bob Peterson/West Stock. 123: Grant Heilman Photography; *inset* Runk/Schoenberger/Grant Heilman Photography. 124: *t.l.* © Carl Purcell/Photo Researchers, Inc.; *m.* © 1987 Michal Heron/Woodfin Camp & Associates; *b.l.* Alfred Zulliger/Shostal Associates. 125: *t.* © James Sobota/West Stock; *b.* Silver Burdett & Ginn. 126: *t.* Galen Rowell/Peter Arnold, Inc.; *b.* © Richard Parker, National Audubon Society Collection/Photo Researchers, Inc. 127: Dan De Wilde for Silver Burdett & Ginn. 128: *t.l.* Phil Degginger; *b.* Silver Burdett & Ginn; *inset* Runk/Schoenberger/Grant Heilman Photography. 129: Dan De Wilde for Silver Burdett & Ginn. 130: NASA. 131: Dan De Wilde for Silver Burdett & Ginn. 132: Eric Carle/Shostal Associates. 133: *t.* Bob McKeenen/Tom Stack & Associates; *b.l., b.m., b.r.* Imagery. 134: E.R. Degginger. 135: Imagery. 136: *t., inset* E.R. Degginger; *m.* Cary Wolinsky/Stock, Boston; *b.* Silver Burdett & Ginn. 137: *t.* Kaz Mori/Taurus Photos; *b.* Stacy Pick/Stock, Boston. 138: *t.* Grant Heilman Photography; *b.* E.R. Degginger. 139: *t.* E.R. Degginger; *b.* Daniel S. Brody/Stock, Boston.

Chapter 8 142: NASA. 142–143: Rod Planck/Tom Stack & Associates. 143: *inset* © Day Williams/Photo Researchers, Inc. 145: Giorgio Gualco/Bruce Coleman; *inset* Kevin Schafer/Tom Stack & Associates. 147: Dan De Wilde for Silver Burdett & Ginn. 153: Silver Burdett & Ginn. 154: Dan De Wilde for Silver Burdett & Ginn. 155: E.R. Degginger. 156: *t.* Silver Burdett & Ginn; *m.* E.R. Degginger; *b.* Cary Wolinsky/Stock, Boston. 157: Carl Iwasaki, *Life Magazine,* © Time, Inc. 158: *t.* NASA; *b.* Steve Smith/Liaison. 159: Dan De Wilde for Silver Burdett & Ginn.

Chapter 9 162: *b.l.* Dan De Wilde for Silver Burdett & Ginn; *t.r.* David Madison/Bruce Coleman; *b.r.* E.R. Degginger. 163: *t.* Eric Simmons/Stock, Boston; *b.* Coco McCoy/Rainbow. 164: Silver Burdett & Ginn. 165: *t.l.* A.F. Sozio/A. Devaney; *b.l.* E.R. Degginger; *t.r.* Breck Kent; *b.r.* © Linda Bartlett/Photo Researchers, Inc. 166: *t.* Phil Degginger; *b.* Owen Franken/Stock, Boston. 167: *t.* Tom Stack & Associates. *b.* © 1987 John Blaustein/Woodfin Camp & Associates. 168: *l.* © Harald Sund; *r.* © Renate Jope/Photo Researchers, Inc. 169: Silver Burdett & Ginn. 170: *t.* Jerry Howard/Stock, Boston; *b.* Peter Southwick/Stock, Boston. 171: *t.* Ken Davis/Tom Stack & Associates; *b.l.* F.T. Wood/Shostal Associates; *b.r.* Owen Franken/Stock, Boston. 172: *l.* Silver Burdett & Ginn; *r.* E.R. Degginger. 173: Dan De Wilde for Silver Burdett & Ginn. 174: *t.* William Eastman III/Tom Stack & Associates; *b.* Charles Palek/Tom Stack & Associates. 175: *t.* Grant Heilman Photography; *inset* Cary Wolinsky/Stock, Boston. 176: *t.* George Lepp/Bruce Coleman; *inset* Don Arms/Tom Stack & Associates; *b.* Michael Malyszko/Stock, Boston; *inset* Ronald Thomas/Taurus Photos. 178: *t.l.* James Somers/Taurus Photos; *b.l.* Cliff Fairfield/Taurus Photos; *t.r.* Rick McIntyre/Tom Stack & Associates. 179: Silver Burdett & Ginn.

Chapter 10 Photos by Dan De Wilde for Silver Burdett & Ginn except as noted. 182: *b.l.* J.G. Smith for Silver Burdett & Ginn. 184: *t.* Alfred Owczarak/Taurus Photos; *b.* Silver Burdett & Ginn. 185: *l., m.* Silver Burdett & Ginn; *t.r.* Michal Heron for Silver Burdett & Ginn; *b.r.* David York/The Stock Shop. 186: Michal Heron for Silver Burdett & Ginn. 187: *t.* Silver Burdett & Ginn; *b.* Richard Braaten for Silver Burdett & Ginn. 188: Michal Heron for Silver Burdett & Ginn. 189: *l.* Silver Burdett & Ginn. 195: John Running/Stock, Boston; *inset* Michal Heron for Silver Burdett & Ginn. 196: Richard Braaten for Silver Burdett & Ginn. 198: *t.* Michal Heron for Silver Burdett & Ginn; *b.* E.R. Degginger. 199–200: Richard Braaten for Silver Burdett & Ginn. 210: *t.l.* Donald Dietz/Stock, Boston; *t.r.* Michal Heron; *b.r.* Mike Mazzaschi/Stock, Boston. 202: Focus on Sports. 203: D.L. Wedeking/West Stock. 204: *t.* Will and Reni McIntyre for Silver Burdett & Ginn; *b.* Michal Heron. 205: Richard Braaten for Silver Burdett & Ginn.

Science in Careers 208–209: Silver Burdett & Ginn.

2 3 4 5 6 7 8 9 10—VH—95 94 93 92 91 90 89 88 87